I0554967

THE MYSTICAL INTERPRETATION

of the ancestry of Our Lord Jesus Christ

St. Aileran,

School of Clonard

Translated by: D.P. Curtin

Dalcassian
Publishing
Company

PHILADELPHIA, PA

ISBN: **978-1-960069-76-4** (Paperback)

Library of Congress Control Number:
Author: Curtin, D.P. (1985-)

Printed by Ingram Content Group, 1 Ingram Blvd, La Vergne, Tennessee

First printing edition 2020.

Introduction

The genealogy of the family of Christ is a long-standing mystery within Christian tradition. The Gospel accounts give us two different styles of descent, found in Matthew 1 and Luke 3 respectively. Various church fathers have attempted to reconcile them into some sense of historical unity. However, this has been relatively fruitless, if for no other reason than that the genealogy rendered by St. Luke is clearly non patrilineal.

St. Aileran is not among those who are attempting to bridge the notable discrepancy between the two accounts. Instead, he draws exclusively upon St. Matthew's account. It is apparent that he must have had some familiarity with the Hebrew language, as all of the names are rendered in their Hebrew meanings. St. Aileran then paired the meaning of the name with a quote from the New Testament. This appears to be done to exemplify that Christ was the fulfillment of the promise of his own ancestry.

Reading between the lines, the text also grants us insight into what monks of the period were reading behind the monastic walls. St. Aileran draws upon multiple sources, notably: Josephus, Philo, St. Jerome, and Origen. All of these would have been the subject to considerable study, particularly at the monastic school where Aileran would spend most of his life.

D.P. Curtin
August 1, 2020
Glen Mills, PA

It seems appropriate for the intellect to explain the names of the genealogy of the Lord next to the mystics, perceived only by the authority of the elders. In that sense, first of all, that the interpretation of each one should be referred to our Lord Jesus as a man and [perhaps, the name], should be supported by the appropriate testimonies of the sacred Scriptures. All generations of the genealogy should be taught as if he had shaped and prophesied the Savior himself, whose genealogies were inserted by divine providence. Therefore, the Lord Jesus Christ, who is a priest according to the order of Melchizedek (*Ps. 19*), and a King according to the election of David, whom Samuel anointed before his brothers as king and prophet (*1 Kings 16:18*). Just as the Father, Jesus Christ, with the oil of joy before his partakers (*Heb. 1:9*), was the Patriarch's patriarch, and the priests' Priest, and the judges' Judge, and the prophets' Prophet, and the leaders' Leader, and apostles' Apostle. Among the angels, he is called the angel of great counsel.

"Abraham " means the exalted Father (*Jerome, Interpretation of the Numbers in GenesisI, 1*), of whom Isaiah speaks among other things: 'His name shall be called Wonderful, Counselor, Mighty God, Father of the future age, Prince of Peace' (*Isaiah 9:6*). And David said: "yet if his children forsake my law, and walk not in my judgments, if they have profaned my righteousness, and have not kept my commandments, I will visit their iniquities with the rod'. (*Ps. 88*) For when the children of our Lord Jesus Christ, whom he begat with the word of life, and caused to be born again by baptism, have fallen. They shall not be joined, because the Lord supplants the hand of his mercy (*Ps. 36:24*) which he extended to the perilous Peter (*Matt. 14:30*).

Isaac rejoiced (*Philo, Interpretation of the Numbers in Genesis, I; Origen. Homily VII on Genesis*); just as the angel said to the shepherds: 'Behold, I announce to you great joy that will be among all the people' (*Luke 2:10*), and as John the Baptist had said to Zechariah: 'And many will rejoice at his birth' (*Luke 1:14*). For prophets and holy men and those born of divine promise, joy arose from parents and relatives. Being born as the Redeemer of all and the Lord of the whole world, an incomparable merit of the greatest joy is announced to all the people, that is to say, to all the human race.

And like Jacob the supplanter (*Gen. 27:36; Origen, Homily 11 on Exodus; Arnobius, On the Psalms, 52*), he indeed says: 'No one can enter a strong man's house and plunder his vessels, unless he first binds the strong man'. (*Matt. 12:29*) For the Lord supplanted Satan when he said: 'Go behind me, Satan!' (*Mark 8:31*) For he pushed the creature back.

And like Judah was confused, (*Jerome., Commentary on Mark III., Interpretations on Matthew; Origen, Homily XVII on Gensis*), it was said: 'I confess to you, Father, Lord of heaven and earth'. (*Matt. 12, 25*)

And just as Pharez divided them all, (*Origen, Homily XXIII on Matthew*) it is He who separates the sheep from the kids (*Matt. 25:32*), that is, the fruitful from the unfruitful.

And Zerah the eastern (*Philo, Interpretations of Genesis, I*), who held the prophetic spirit: 'Behold', he said, 'the Man of the East is his name'. Of which Zechariah also says: 'The East visited us from on high (*Zech. 6:12; Luke 1:78*). And elsewhere: 'To those who fear the name of the Lord, the sun of justice will rise, and health will be in his feathers (*Malachi 4:2*). Abraham desired to see the rising and setting of the day, and he saw it (*John 8:56*). We must, therefore, have the understanding that the origin of life, in which the Word became flesh and dwelt among us (*John 1:14*), and the setting of the death on the cross, which he suffered for us (*Phil. 2:8*). For that eternal and ineffable day of Divinity, of which it is said: 'Today I have begotten thee' (*Ps. 19:4*). And this is always the beginning, but knows no rising. There is always an end, but it has no setting. Coccini [Forte, Coccini], however, is a term derived from the Lord in such a way that it signifies either the blood-red of passion, or of burning charity (of which he gave as an example), and the unquenchable ardor in him.

As for Esdron- He saw an arrow (*Origin. Homily XXXV on Matthew; Augustine, Supplement on the Psalms, 87; Hesychius, Supplements to Leviticus, XIV*), or his court (*Philo, Interpretations of Joshua, I*), to which it is said: 'The sharp arrows of the mighty' (*Ps. 19:4*) His arrows are the precepts of the Lord, or the judgments of the judge. Yet, the court, that is, the house wide and open to all, is therefore called, because inviting all to him he says: 'Come to me, all you who labor and are heavy laden' (*Matt. 11:28*), and again: 'Go, he says, to the exits of the roads, and compel all to enter'. (*Luke 14:23*)

As for Aram the Elect, of whom he thus speaks: 'Behold my Child, whom I have chosen, my elect, I have given my spirit upon him' (*Matt. 12:18*). We might ask who is the chosen child, except He who from childhood rejected evil and chose what is good. (*Isaiah 7:13*) As this is not common to all children, except one child, who was born of sin, without sin, like a rotten worm from putrefaction.

As for Aminadab, my spontaneous people (*Philo, Integration on Exodus, Numbers, and Judges, I*), who said: 'No one has life except through me' (*John 10:18*), and: 'If you want to come to life, keep the commandments'. (*Matt. 19:17*).

As for Nahason who prophesied, (*Jerome., Interpretation of the Book of Hebrews, Acts of the Apostles, and Matthew*), with many promises, saying: 'When the Son of man comes in his majesty' (*Luke 9:26*), and whose prophecy he saw in the three times of prophecy, in the past, as it is, Abraham saw in his day, and was glad. He saw in the present, as it is currently, for: 'What evil thoughts do you think in your hearts?' (*John 8:56*) In the future, as it will be: 'For they will be like angels in heaven'. (Matthew 9:4) Moreover, that: 'Dismantle this temple, and in three days I will raise it up'. (*John 2:19*)

As for Salmon the sensible (*Jerome, Interpretations on Matthew; Mark 12:25*), who said: 'Someone touched me, for I felt that strength had gone out of me (*Luke 8:46*), and: 'Why do you think evil in your hearts?' (*Matt. 9:4*) He truly has perceptive who sees thoughts as facts, and futures as present. Just as it is written about him: 'He made the things that are to come'. (*Wis. 8:8*)

As for Boaz, in whom there is strength (*Philo, Interpretations of the Book of Judith and Ruth*) who said: 'I will draw all things to myself'. (*John 12:32*) All man's virtue fails in death, but the Word, which was made flesh, became stronger from infirmity, more alive from death, more exalted from humility.

As for Obed the servant (*Josephus, Antiquities, 5.14*), who did not come to be ministered to, but to minister (*Matt. 20:28*); likewise the apostle said: 'He took the form of a servant.' (*Phil. 2:7*)

Jesse the perfumed (Philo, Interpretation of 1dt and 3rd Kings), who said: 'I have come to send fire on the earth'. (*Luke 12:49*) And John himself said: 'He will baptize you in the Holy Spirit and fire'. (*Matt. 3:11; Luke 3*)

As for the beloved David (*Jerome, Interpretations on Matthew and Acts of the Apostles*) of whom the evangelist says: 'And his face shone like the sun'. (*Matt. 17:2*) Where also the Prophet had said: 'A beautiful form before the sons of men'. (*Ps. 44:3*)

As for Solomon the peacemaker (*Origen, Homily VI on John*), who said: 'My peace I give you'. (*John 14:27*) Adding mine shows that he hates not his own. Of which it is said: 'I did not come to send peace on earth, but a sword'. (*Matt. 10:34*) And as the Apostle of Christ says: 'He is our peace, who made both one'. (*Eph. 2:14*)

As for Rehoboam, who was the father of the people (*Philo, Interpretations on 2 Kings; Jerome, Commentary on Matthew*), when he says: 'Many will come from the East and the West, and recline with Abraham and Isaac and Jacob in the kingdom of heaven'. (*Matt. 8*) And also elsewhere: 'Come unto me, all ye that labor and are heavy laden' (*Matt. 11:28*), and the movement of the people is therefore called, because as lightning comes from the East and shines even to the West, so will the coming of the Son of Man be (*Matt. 24:27*).

As for Abia, the Father is the Lord (*Jerome, Commentary on Matthew*), who said: 'Do not call yourselves Father on earth (*Matt. 23:9*), not because we say that there are two in the Godhead, but because the teacher of a man is also the father of that man who is taught, as Paul says: 'For even if you have ten thousand teachers in Christ, but only one father, for I have begotten you in Christ Jesus through the Gospel (*1 Cor. 4*). If the disciple deserved to be called father, how much more his Master.

As for Asa taking away (*Philo, Commentary on Jeremiah and Kings III*), about which John: 'Behold, he says, the Lamb of God, which takes away sins'. (*John 1:29*)

As for Josaphat himself judging (*Philo, Commentary on Kings II & III*), as he says: The Father judges no one, but has given all judgment to the Son. (*John 5:22*)

As for Joram, where he is exalted (*Philo, Commentary on Kings, III; Jerome, Commentary on Matthew*), as he said: 'No one ascends into heaven, except he who descends from heaven.' (*John 3:13*)

As for Uzziah, the strong man of the Lord (*Philo, Commentary on Isaiah*), who said: 'Lazarus, come out (*John 11:43*). Then indeed the voice of the Lord was in power, when he raised the soul of the four-day dead from hell, and the body from the grave.

As for Jotham, when he was finished (*Jerome, Commentary on Hebrew Matthew*), of whom it is said: 'Finished with every temptation.' (*Luke 4:13*) and at the end of all that was prophesied concerning him it is said: 'And when he had finished. Then he said all these words to his disciples: You know that after two days the Passover will take place.' (*Matt. 26:2*) And hanging on the cross and having drunk vinegar, he said: 'It is finished, and bowing his head he gave up the ghost'. (*John 19:30*) If it is said that he is perfect (the author of the imperfect work, *Homily I on Matthew*), it is explained in this way, because he commands his own to be perfect, saying: 'Be perfect, even as your heavenly Father is perfect'. (*Matt. 5:48*) Jesus ought to have been called perfect above all others, seeing that he began to do and to teach (*Acts 1:1*) those things which are perfect.

Turning to Ahaz (*Anonymous, Homily on Matthew I; Origen, Commentary on Exodus*), who said: 'Do penance, for the kingdom of heaven is near' (*Matt. 3:2*). or by grasping (*Philo, Interpretations of Micah*), took hold of his hand, and healed Peter's mother-in-law who was feverish (*Luke 4:38*). He thereafter raised the dead daughter of the prince (*Matt. 9:23*). Paul also said: 'by what means, do I apprehend in which I am apprehended?' (*Phil. 3:12*). Also elsewhere he said: 'For he did not take hold of angels, but he took hold of the seed of Abraham'. (*Heb. 22:16*)

The Lord strengthened Hezekiah (*Anonymous, Homily on Matthew I*), who said: 'Trust me, I have overcome the world' (*John 16:31*). And Paul said: 'But we, he says, preach that Christ is the power of God and the wisdom of God.' (*1 Cor. 1, 24*)

As for Manasseh the forgetful (*Philo, Commentary on Genesis*), who said: 'Many sins are forgiven him, because he loved much' (*Luke 7:47*) for 'charity covers a multitude of sinners'. (*James 5:20*) And Ezekiel said: 'On whatever day, he says, the unrighteous man turns from his unrighteousness, all his iniquities will be forgotten'. (*Ezek. 18*)

As for Ammon the faithful (*Philo, Commentary on Jeremiah*), who said: 'Ask and it will be given to you' (*Matt. 7:7*). And Paul said: 'That he might become a merciful and faithful priest to the Lord'. (*Heb. 2:17*) And John in the Apocalypse: 'And from Jesus Christ, who is a faithful witness' (*Rev. 1:5*). Yet, he is said to be faithful, whose promises are always faithful, which are equally to be hoped for and to be feared on both sides.

As for Josiah where there is incense of the Lord (*Jerome, Commentary on Hebrews*), of which it was said: 'And he prayed at length' (*Luke 22:44*), but how prayer is said to be incense, as the Psalmist testifies, saying: 'Let my prayer be directed, O Lord, as incense in your sight'. (*Ps. 140:2*)

As for Jechoniah who was preparing (*Jerome, Commentary on Hebrew; Philo, Commentary on 1 Kings and Jeremiah*), as he said: 'If I go and prepare a place for you, I will come to you again and receive you to myself'. (*John 14:3*)

As for Jechoniah and Joachim, that is, the father and son, as they should be distinguished. In Joachim the resurrection of the Lord is said (*Jerome, Commentary on Matthew*): 'But after I have risen, I will go before you into Galilee'. (*Matt. 26:2*) In Joachim is the preparation of the Lord (*Author of the imperfect work, Homily I on Matthew*), who said: 'Come, blessed of my Father, inherit the kingdom prepared for you from the beginning of the world'. (*Matt. 25:34*)

In Salathiel, my request is to God (*Jerome, Commentary on Matthew; Philo, Commentary on Haggai*), who said: 'Holy Father, keep those whom you have given me'. (*John 17:11*)

In Zerubbabel himself the teacher of confusion (*Jerome, Commentary on Matthew*), as he said: 'Many will come from the East and the West and recline with Abraham and Isaac and Jacob in the kingdom of heaven'. (*Matthew 8:11*) And of the same it is said: 'Why does your Master eat with publicans and sinners?' (*Mark 2:16*)

As for Abiud, this is my Father (*Philo, Commentary on Exodus*), who said: 'I and my Father are one'. (*John 10:30*)

The Lord will raise up Eliachim (*Philo, Commentary on the Book of Kings*), as he said: 'He who believes in me will not die forever, but I will raise him up at the last day'. (*John 6:40*)

As for Azor, he was helped (*Philo , Introduction for Kings III & Jeremiah)*, as he said: 'I am not alone, because the Father is with me' (*John 8:19*)

As for Sadoch justified (*Jerome, Introduction to Luke*), as he said: 'I speak the truth, because he who sent me is true'. (*John 8:26*) To whom it was also said: 'You are justified in your words'. (*Ps. 5:6*) And as John says, 'We have an advocate with the Father, Jesus Christ the righteous'. (*John 2:1*)

As for Achim, my brother (*Origin. Homily XX about the Nativity of Christ*), as he said: 'Whoever does the will of my Father, he is my brother, and my mother, and sister', (*Matt. 12:50*) or mother's brother. For the Lord is therefore called the brother of his mother, while there is one Father, to whom we all (by commanding Christ) say: 'Our Father who art in heaven.'

As for Eliud this is my God (*Philo, Introduction to I Kings*), to whom Thomas says: 'My Lord and my God' (*John 20:28*). But this pronoun signifies nothing but the signs of nails and lances, which show the knowledge of the body of truth.

As for Eleazar, God is my helper (*Philo, Commentary on Genesis and Exodus*), as he says: 'And the Father who sent me is with me' (*John 8:16*).

Charity is Mathan (*Jerome, Commentary on Matthew*), as he said: 'All debt will be given to you because you asked me' (*Matt. 18:32*)

As for Jacob. the supplanter (*Origen, Homily XI on Exodus*), as he said: 'I have given you power to tread on serpents and scorpions, and over all the power of the enemy'. (*Luke 10:1*)

In Joseph it was increased, or added to (*Philo, Commentary on Genesis; Josephus, Antiquities, 1.7*), so that he said: 'I came that they may have life, and let them have it more abundantly'. (*John 10:10*) Elsewhere he said 'I have other sheep, which are not of this fold, and I must bring them, that there may be one flock and one Shepherd'. (*John 10:1*)

So far as we have been able, we have affirmed the manner in which Christ was represented and prophesied in all the genealogies, or generations [perhaps, the steps of the generations], by the examples of the Holy Scriptures.

LATIN TEXT

Interpretatio mystica

Opportunum videtur de nominibus genealogiae dominicae juxta mysticos, majorum duntaxat auctoritate perceptos, exponere intellectus; eo utique sensu imprimis posito, ut quomodo in Dominum nostrum Jesum hominis [Forte, nominis] cujusque referenda sit interpretatio, convenientibus sacrarum Scripturarum astruatur testimoniis, ipsumque Salvatorem omnes genealogiae generationes figurasse ac prophetasse doceantur, cujus genealogiae divina providentia sunt insertae. Dominus itaque Jesus Christus, qui est Sacerdos secundum ordinem Melchisedech (Psal. CIX), et Rex secundum electionem David, quem unxit Samuel prae fratribus suis in regem et prophetam (I Reg. XVI, 18), sicut etiam Pater, Jesum Christum oleo laetitiae prae participibus suis (Hebr. I, 9), in [qui in] patriarchis Patriarcha, in sacerdotibus Sacerdos, in judicibus Judex, in prophetis Propheta, in ducibus Dux, in apostolis Apostolus; in angelis, magni consilii Angelus dicitur.

In Abraham Pater excelsus intelligitur (Hieron. l. Interp. nom. Hebr., de Gen.), de quo inter caetera Isaias loquitur: Vocabitur nomen ejus Admirabilis, Consiliarius, Deus Fortis, Pater futuri saeculi, Princeps pacis (Isai. IX, 6). Et David inquit: Si autem dereliquerint filii ejus legem meam, et in judiciis meis non ambulaverint; si justitias meas profanaverint, et mandata mea non custodierint, visitabo in virga iniquitates eorum (Psal. LXXXVIII). Cum enim ceciderint filii Domini nostri Jesu Christi, quos verbo vitae genuit, et per baptismum iterum nasci fecit, non collidentur; quia Dominus supponit manum misericordiae suae (Psal. XXXVI, 24) quam periclitanti Petro porrexit (Matth. XIV, 30).

In Isaac gaudium (Philo, l. Interp. nom. Hebr., de Genes., Origen. homil. 7 in Gen.); dicente angelo ad pastores: Ecce annuntio vobis gaudium magnum, quod erit in omni populo (Luc. II, 10), nam ut de Joanne Baptista dixerat ad Zachariam: Et multi in nativitate ejus gaudebunt (Luc. I, 14). Prophetis namque et sanctis hominibus et divina repromissione nascentibus, gaudium parentibus oriebatur et propinquis; nascente autem omnium Redemptore ac totius mundi Domino, merito incomparabile et maximum gaudium omni populo, id est, omni humano generi annuntiatur exortum.

In Jacob supplantator (Gen. XXVII, 36. Origen. hom. 11 in Exod. Arnob., in Psalm. LII) ipse etenim dicit: Nemo potest in domum fortis introire, et vasa ejus diripere, nisi prius alligaverit fortem (Matth. XII, 29); supplantatum enim Dominus habuit Satanam, cum dixerit: Vade retro, Satanas (Marc. VIII, 31); plantam [Forte, planta] namque retro retrudit.

In Juda confitens (Hieron., in c. III Marc., et l. Interp. nom. de Matth.; Orig., hom. 17 in Gen.), qui dixit: Confiteor tibi, Pater Domine coeli et terrae (Matth. XII, 25).

In Phares Divisor (Origen., hom. 23 in Matth.) qui separat oves ab haedis (Matth. XXV, 32), id est, fructuosos ab infructuosis.

In Zara Orientalis (Philo, l. Interp. nom. de Gen.), de quo prophetalis spiritus: Ecce, inquit, Vir Oriens nomen ejus. De quo item Zacharias ait: Visitavit nos Oriens ex alto (Zach. VI, 12; Luc. I, 78). Et alibi: Timentibus nomen Domini orietur sol justitiae, et sanitas in pennis ejus (Malach. IV, 2); cujus diei ortum et occasum videre concupivit Abraham, et vidit (Joan. VIII, 56). Ortum autem nativitatem, qua Verbum caro factum est, et habitavit in nobis (Joan. I, 14), occasum vero mortem crucis, quam passus est pro nobis (Phil. II, 8), intelligere debemus. Ille enim aeternus et inneffabilis Divinitatis dies, de quo dicitur: Hodie genui te (Psal. CIX, 4), semper est principium, sed nescit ortum; semper est finis, sed nullum habens occasum. Coccinei [Forte, Coccini] autem sic a Domino derivatur vocabulum, ut vel rubrum passionis cruorem, vel ignitae charitatis (cujus exemplum dedit), inexstinguibilem in ipso significat ardorem.

In Esdron. Sagittam vidit (Origen. hom. 35 sup. Matth.; Aug., sup. psalm. LXXXVII; Isych., sup. Levit. XIV), sive atrium ejus (Philo, l. Interp. hom., de Josue), cui dicitur: Sagittae potentis acutae (Psal. CXIX, 4); sagittae autem ipsius praecepta sunt dominica, vel judicantis judicia: Atrium vero, id est, domus lata et omnibus patens, idcirco dicitur, eo quod omnes ad se invitans dicit: Venite ad me, omnes qui laboratis et onerati estis (Matth. XI, 28): Itemque qui manet in me et ego in illo, hic fert fructum multum (Joan. XV, 5); et iterum: Ite, inquit, ad exitus viarum, et compellite omnes intrare (Luc. XIV, 23).

In Aram Electus de quo sic loquitur. Ecce Puer meus, quem elegi, electus meus, dedi spiritum meum super eum (Matth. XII, 18); et revera quis est puer electus, nisi qui a pueritia reprobavit malum et elegit quod bonum est (Isai. VII, 13); quod non est commune omnium puerorum, praeter unum puerum, qui de peccato, sine peccato, ut vermis imputridus de putredine natus est.

In Aminadab Populus meus spontaneus (Philo, l. Interp. nom., de Exod., Num., Judic.), qui dicit: Nemo tollit animam meam a me ipso (Joan. X, 18). Et: Si vis in vitam venire, serva mandata (Matth. XIX, 17).

In Naason augurans (Hieron., l. Interp. nom. Hebr., ae Actis apost., et Matth.), qui promittit dicens: Cum venerit Filius hominis in majestate sua (Luc. IX, 26), cujus prophetia in tria prophetiae tempora respexit, in praeteritum, ut est, vidit Abraham diem [meum], et gavisus est; in praesens, ut est: Quid cogitatis mala in cordibus vestris (Joan. VIII, 56)? In futurum, ut est: Erunt enim sicut angeli in coelo (Matth. IX, 4); et illud: Solvite templum hoc, et in tribus diebus excitabo [illud] (Joan. II, 19).

In Salomon sensibilis (Hier. l. Interp. nom. de Matth.); Marc. XII, 25, qui dicit: Tetigit me aliquis, nam ego sensi virtutem de me exisse (Luc. VIII, 46). Et: Quid cogitatis mala in cordibus vestris (Matth. IX, 4)? Vere sensibilis est, qui cogitata ut facta, et futura ut praesentia cernit; sicut de eo scriptum est: Qui fecit quae futura sunt (Sap. VIII, 8).

In Booz in quo robur est (Philo, l. Interp. nom., de lib. Judic., Ruth) qui ait: Omnia traham ad meipsum (Joan. XII, 32). Omnis hominis virtus in morte deficit, Verbum vero quod caro factum est, de infirmitate fortius, de morte vivacius, de humilitate excelsius factum est.

In Obed serviens (Joseph, l. V, c. 14, Ant.), qui non venit ministrari, sed ministrare (Matth. XX, 28); itemque Apostolus: Formam, inquit, servi accepit (Philipp. II, 7).

In Jesse incensum (Philo, l. Interp., de I et III Reg.) qui ait: Ignem veni mittere in terram (Luc. XII, 49). Et Joannes: ipse, ait: Baptizabit vos in Spiritu sancto et igni (Matth. III, 11; Luc. III).

In David desiderabilis (Hieron. l. Int. nom., de Matth.; et Act. apost.), de quo evangelista dicit: Et resplenduit facies ejus sicut sol (Matth. XVII, 2). Unde etiam Propheta dixerat: Speciosus forma prae filiis hominum (Psal. XLIV, 3).

In Salomone pacificus (Orig. hom. 6 in Joan.), qui ait: Pacem meam do vobis (Joan. XIV, 27). Addens meam ostendit odisse non suam; de qua dicitur: Non veni pacem mittere in terram, sed gladium (Matth. X, 34). Et Apostolus de Christo: Ipse, inquit, est pax nostra qui fecit utraque unum (Ephes. II, 14).

In Roboam latitudo populi (Philo, l. Int. nom., de II Reg.; Hieron., ibid., de Matth.), cum ait: Multi ab Oriente et Occidente venient, et recumbent cum Abraham et Isaac et Jacob in regno coelorum (Matth. VIII). Itemque alibi: Venite ad me, omnes qui laboratis et onerati estis (Matth. XI, 28), impetus autem populi idcirco vocatur, quia sicut fulgur exit ab Oriente et paret usque in Occidentem, ita erit et adventus Filii hominis (Matth. XXIV, 27).

In Abia Pater Dominus (Hieron, ubi supra, de Matth.), qui ait: Nolite vocare vobis Patrem super terram (Matth. XXIII, 9), non quia duos in divinitate dicamus esse, sed quod etiam homo magistri illius hominis pater sit quem docet, Paulo dicente: Nam etsi decem millia paedagogorum habeatis in Christo, sed non multos patres; nam in CHRISTO JESU per Evangelium ego vos genui (I Cor. 4). Si autem discipulus meruit pater vocari, quanto magis Magister ejus.

In Asa tollens (Philo, l. Int. nom, de III Reg., Jeremia), de quo Joannes: Ecce, inquit, Agnus Dei, qui tollit peccata (Joan. I, 29).

In Josaphat ipse judicans (Philo, ibid, Reg. II, III), ut ait: Pater non judicat quemquam, sed omne judicium dedit Filio (Joan. V, 22).

In Joram ubi est excelsus (Philo, ibid., Reg. III; Hieron., ibid., de Matth.), ut ait: Nemo ascendit in coelum, nisi qui de coelo descendit (Joan. III, 13).

In Ozia robustus Domini (Philo, ibid., de Esaia), qui dixit: Lazare, prodi foras (Joan. XI, 43). Tunc etenim vox Domini fuit in virtute, cum animam quatriduani mortui ab inferis, et corpus revocavit de sepulcro.

In Joatham consummatus (Hieron. l. Int. nom. Heb., de Matth.), de quo dicitur: Consummata omni tentatione (Luc. IV, 13); et in fine omnium, quae prophetata sunt de eo dicitur: Et cum consummasset. Tunc omnia verba haec dixit discipulis suis: Scitis quia post biduum pascha fiet (Matth. XXVI, 2). Et in cruce pendens acetoque potatus dixit: Consummatum est, et inclinato capite tradidit spiritum (Joan. XIX, 30). Si vero perfectus (Auctor oper. imperf., hom. 1 in Matth.) dicatur, sic exponitur, quia qui suos jubet esse perfectos, dicens: Estote perfecti, sicut et Pater vester coelestis perfectus est (Matth. V, 48); prae caeteris perfectus dici debuit Jesus, quippe qui coepit facere et docere (Act. I, 1) quae perfecta sunt.

In Achaz convertens (Auctor op. imperf., hom. 1 in Matth., et Orig., in Ex.), qui ait: Poenitentiam agite, appropinquavit enim regnum coelorum (Matth. III, 2); vel apprehendens (Philo, l. Int. nom. de Michaea), qui apprehensa manu socrum Petri sanavit febricitantem (Luc. IV, 38), et filiam principis mortuam resuscitavit (Matth. IX, 23). Paulus quoque: Si quo modo, inquit, apprehendam in quo apprehensus sum (Philipp. III, 12). Item alibi: Non enim angelos apprehendit, sed semen Abrahae apprehendit (Hebr. XXII, 16).

In Ezechia confortavit Dominus (Auctor. anonym., hom. 1 in Matth.), qui ait: Confidite, ego vici mundum (Joan. XVI, 31). Et Paulus: Nos autem, ait, praedicamus: Christum Dei virtutem et Dei sapientiam (I Cor. I, 24).

In Manasse obliviosus (Philo, ubi supra de Genes.), qui ait: Remittuntur ei peccata multa, quia dilexit multum (Luc. VII, 47); Charitas namque multitudinem operit peccatorum (Jac. V, 20). Et Ezechiel: In quacunque die, ait, conversus fuerit injustus ab injustitia sua, omnes iniquitates ejus oblivioni tradentur (Ezech. XVIII).

In Amon fidelis (Philo, ibid., de Jerem.), qui ait: Petite et dabitur vobis (Matth. VII, 7). Et Paulus ait; Ut misericors fieret, et fidelis Pontifex ad Dominum (Hebr. II, 17). Et Joannes in Apocalypsi: Et a Jesu Christo, qui est testis fidelis (Apoc. I, 5); fidelis autem dicitur, cujus sunt semper promissa fidelia, quae in utramque partem et speranda sunt pariter, et expavescenda.

In Josia ubi est incensum Domini (Hier. l. interp. nom. Hebr.), de quo dicitur: Et prolixius orabat (Luc. XXII, 44), quomodo vero oratio incensum esse dicitur, Psalmista testatur, dicens: Dirigatur, Domine, oratio mea sicut incensum in conspectu tuo (Psal. CXL, 2).

In Jechonia praeparans (Hieron., ibid.; et Philo, 4. Interp. nom., de I Reg. et Jerem.), ut ait: Si abiero et praeparavero vobis locum, iterum veniam ad vos, et accipiam vos ad meipsum (Joan. XIV, 3).

Si vero proprie Joachim, et Joachin, id est, Pater, distinguatur; in Joachin Domini resurrectio dicitur (Hieron., ibid. de Matth.), ut ait: Postquam autem resurrexero, praecedam vos in Galilaeam (Matth. XXVI, 2); in Joachim Domini praeparatio (Auctor oper. imperf., hom. 1 in Matth.), qui dixit: Venite, benedicti Patris mei, possidete paratum vobis regnum ab origine mundi (Matth. XXV, 34).

In Salathiel, petitio mea Deus (Hieron., ibid., de Matth.; Philo, ibid., de Aggaeo), qui dixit: Pater sancte, serva eos quos dedisti mihi (Joan. XVII, 11).

In Zorobabel ipse magister confusionis (Hieron., ibid.), ut ait: Multi ab Oriente et Occidente venient et recumbent cum Abraham et Isaac et Jacob in regno coelorum (Matth. VIII, 11); et de eodem dicitur: Quare cum Publicanis et peccatoribus manducat Magister vester (Marc. II, 16)?

In Abiud Pater meus iste (Philo, ibid., Exod.), qui dicit: Ego et Pater meus unum sumus (Joan. X, 30).

In Eliachim Dominus resuscitabit (Philo, ibid., de lib. Reg.), ut ait: Qui credit in me non morietur in aeternum, sed resuscitabo eum in novissimo die (Joan. VI, 40).

In Azor, adjutus (Philo l. Int. nom., de III Reg. Jeremia), ut ait: Non sum solus, quia Pater mecum est (Joan. VIII, 19).

In Sadoch justificatus (Hieron. l. Int. nom., de Luca), ut ait: Ego veritatem loquor, quia verax est qui me misit (Joan. VIII, 26); ad quem etiam dicitur: Justificeris in sermonibus tuis (Psal. L, 6). Et Joannes: Advocatum, inquit habemus apud Patrem Jesum Christum justum (Joan. II, 1).

In Achim Frater meus (Origen. hom. 20 supra Jesu Nave), ut ait: Quicunque fecerit voluntatem Patris mei, ipse frater meus, et mater mea, et soror est (Matth. XII, 50), sive frater matris; frater quippe matris Dominus ideo dicitur, dum unum Patrem, cui omnes (Christo jubente) dicimus: Pater noster qui es in coelis (Ibid.).

In Eliud Deus meus iste (Philo, l. Int. nom., de l. I Reg.), cui Thomas ait: Dominus et Deus meus (Joan. XX, 28). Pronomen autem iste quid aliud nisi signa clavorum et lanceae significat, quae veri notitiam corporis monstrant.

In Eleazar Deus meus adjutor (Philo, l. Int. nom., de Gen. et Ex.), ut ait: Et qui misit me Pater mecum est (Joan. VIII, 16).

In Mathan donans (Hieron. l. Int. nom., de Matth.), ut ait: Omne debitum donari tibi quia rogasti me (Matth. XVIII, 32).

In Jacob supplantator (Origen., hom. 11 in Exod.), ut ait: Dedi vobis potestatem calcandi super serpentes, et scorpiones, et supra omnem virtutem inimici (Luc. X).

In Joseph auctus, vel apponens (Philo, ibid., de Genes.; Joseph. l. I, c. 17, Antiq.), ut ait: Ego veni, ut vitam habeant; et abundantius habeant (Joan. X, 10); et alibi; et alias oves habeo, quae non sunt ex hoc ovili, et illas oportet me adducere, ut fiat unus grex et unus Pastor (Joan. X).

Hactenus ut valuimus, qualiter in omnibus genealogiae, vel generationibus [Forte, generationis gradibus] Christus figuratus et prophetatus sit, exemplis sacrae Scripturae asseruimus.

The Scriptorium Project is the work of a small group of lay people of various apostolic churches who are interested in the preservation, transmission, and translation of the works of the early and medieval church. Our efforts are to make the works of the church fathers accessible to anyone who might have an interest in Christian antiquities and the theological, philosophical, and moral writings that have become the bedrock of Western Civilization.

To-date, our releases have pulled from the Greek, Syriac, Georgian, Latin, Celtic, Ethiopian, and Coptic traditions of Christianity, and have been pulled from sundry local traditions and languages.

Other Titles and Translations by D.P. Curtin:

First Book of Ethiopian Maccabees (2018)
Protoevangelium of James: Greek and English Texts (2019)
Edicts of the Synod of Paris by Chlothar II, King of Franks (2019)
The Life of St. Desiderius by Sisebut, King of Visigoths (2019)
The Synod of Rome by St. Boniface IV of Rome (2019)
Letter to Pope Theodore by Victor of Carthage (2020)
The Decree of 610 by Gundemar, King of Visigoths (2020)
Laws of the Church by Chlothar III, King of Franks (2020)
Donations by St. Aethelbert, King of Kent (2020)
The Mystical Interpretation by St. Aileran the Wise (2020)
Laws of the Church by St. Dagobert II, King of Franks (2020)
The Old Nubian Miracle of St. Mena (2021)
About Fifteen Problems by St. Albertus Magnus (2022)
Testament of Some Former Things by John Scotus Eriugena (2022)
The Georgian Synaxarium (2022)
Instructions: Counsel for Novices by St. Ammonas the Hermit (2022)
The Syriac Menologium and Martyrology (2022)
Book on Religious Exercise and Quiet by St. Isaiah the Solitary (2022)
Vision of Theophilus by St. Cyril of Alexandria (2022)
On Fate (De Fato) by St. Albertus Magnus (2023)
Fragments of 'Chronicle' by Hippolytus of Thebes (2023)
Life of the Blessed Theotokos by Epiphanius Monachus (2023)
Syriac Life of John the Baptist by Serapion the Presbyter (2023)
Second Book of Ethiopian Maccabees (2023)